MAKE MONEY!

BE A PET SITTER

Bridget Heos **Illustrated by Daniele Fabbri**

Amicus Illustrated is published by Amicus
P.O. Box 1329, Mankato, MN 56002
www.amicuspublishing.us

Library of Congress Cataloging-in-Publication Data
Heos, Bridget.
 Make money! Be a pet sitter / by Bridget Heos ;
illustrated by Daniele Fabbri.
     pages cm. — (Make money!)
 Summary: "Through trial and error and a few
humorous mistakes, a girl learns how to take care of
pets, find clients, and create a successful pet sitting
business to earn enough money to buy her own pet"—
Provided by publisher.
 Includes bibliographical references.
 ISBN 978-1-60753-362-7 (library binding) – ISBN
978-1-60753-410-5 (ebook)
 1. Pet sitting–Juvenile literature. I. Fabbri, Daniele,
1978- illustrator. II. Title. III. Title: Be a pet sitter.
 SF414.34.H46 2014
 636.088'7—dc23

                                    2012050607

Editor: Rebecca Glaser
Designer: The Design Lab

Printed in the United States of America at
Corporate Graphics in North Mankato, Minnesota.

Date 2/2013   PO 1147

10 9 8 7 6 5 4 3 2 1

So you want a guinea pig? It costs $15. You also need a cage, bedding, and food. That adds up to $80! Your mom says you have to earn it. But how?

You love animals, right? You could be a pet sitter. You may already have some pet friends. Offer to take your favorite furry pal for a walk.

Did you tell the owner what you charge? She thought you were walking the dog just for fun. It is fun. But you're also saving for a pet.

You asked your parents, right? Will they help if you need it? Can pets stay at your house?

"Yes," says Mom. "As long as you remember that it's mainly your job. Because I already have a job."

Time to pass out your flyer. The pet store lets you post one there.

The phone rings. Your first customer! Mr. Ortega wants you to walk his dog. Don't forget a baggy for when doggy has to go. (And perhaps a clothespin for your nose.)

Look, Mrs. Schmidt is waving. She didn't know you walked dogs.

Of course, you can walk her adorable puppy! Should you walk two at the same time?

Probably not. Come back after you bring the first dog home.

Now you walk these two dogs every weekday. The money is adding up. And the slobbery kisses.

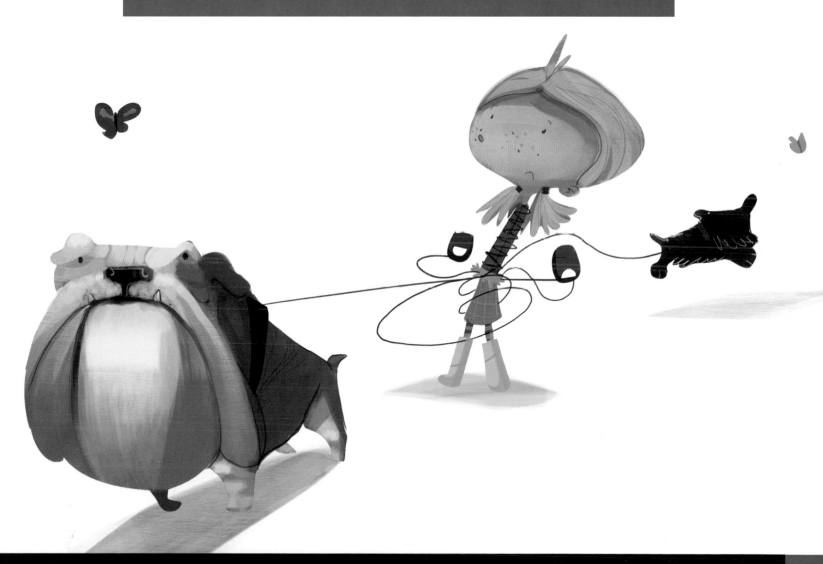

Mr. Sullivan saw your flyer. He asks for references, so you give him Mrs. Schmidt's phone number. She knows you do a good job. After talking to her, Mr. Sullivan hires you to take care of his parrot for five days.

What do you know about parrots? Ask the owner what to feed the bird, how often, and how much. Is the bird allowed out of the cage?

This bird has some instructions of his own. Be sure to follow the owner's rules.

Mrs. Schmidt wants you to watch her puppy in your home for two days. Puppies like to play. Ask Mrs. Schmidt to bring his favorite toys.

Another satisfied customer! And another $20. You've reached your goal!

Business is booming. But you have other responsibilities. Like homework. And now . . . your new guinea pig! She's cute, but she needs to be trained.

It's okay to turn down some jobs. But don't quit working. You'll still need to buy food.

Besides, you would miss your old buddies.
And maybe they'd like to meet your new friend.

Counting Your Money!

If you start pet sitting, keep track of how much you make. Here's a sample based on this story.

DOG WALKS
($2 per walk)
Mr. Ortega's dog (10 walks) $20.00
Mrs. Schmidt's puppy (10 walks) $20.00

FEEDING ANIMALS
($5 per day)
Mr. Sullivan's parrot (5 days) $25.00

DOGSITTING AT YOUR HOUSE
($10 per day)
Mrs. Schmidt's puppy (2 days) $20.00

TOTAL $85.00

Glossary

business Making money by selling goods or doing services.

customers The people who buy or might buy what you're selling.

flyer A piece of paper sharing information, such as about a business.

instructions Steps for completing a job.

reference A person who knows that you do a good job and agrees to share that with others.

responsibilities Actions one must do in order to take care of someone or something.

Read More

Antill, Sara. *10 Ways I Can Earn Money.* New York: PowerKids Press, 2012.

Orr, Tamra. *A Kid's Guide to Earning Money.* Hockessin, Del.: Mitchell Lane, 2009.

Scheunemann, Pam. *Cool Jobs for Young Pet Lovers: Ways to Make Money Caring for Pets.* Edina, Minn.: Abdo, 2011.

Websites

ASPCA Kids
http://www.aspca.org/aspcakids/
Learn about pet care, animal issues, and animal careers

Money for Kids: Making Money
http://www.kidsmoney.org/makemone.htm
Read advice from other kids who have tried earning money.

PBS Kids.org: It's My Life: Money
http://pbskids.org/itsmylife/money/
Learn how to earn, save, and spend wisely.

About the Author

Bridget Heos is the author of more than 30 books for children, but made her millions babysitting in grade school and high school. She once babysat for a parrot who loved watching T.V. He would say, "Turn on Nick at Nite!"

About the Illustrator

Daniele Fabbri was born in Ravenna, Italy, in 1978. He graduated from Istituto Europeo di Design in Milan, Italy, and started his career as cartoon animator, storyboarder, and background designer for animated series. He has worked as a freelance illustrator since 2003, collaborating with international publishers and advertising agencies.